More Praise for *Oubliettes of Light*

The poems in Lisa Ashley's debut collection are knock-your-socks-off good. They are simultaneously lyrical and narrative. The stories are dramatic but are told delicately, with a crystalline economy of words. The poems hit home in the heart and their wisdom remains there. As Ashley says, "There is no such thing as a whole story" yet these poems tell a story so beautifully as to make the reader feel whole.
—Lillo Way, author of *Lend Me Your Wings*

Oubliettes of Light

Oubliettes of Light

Poems

Lisa Ashley

MoonPath Press

Copyright © 2025 Lisa Ashley
All rights reserved.

No part of this publication may be reproduced, distributed, or transmitted in any form or by any means whatsoever without written permission from the publisher, except in the case of brief excerpts for critical reviews and articles. All inquiries should be addressed to MoonPath Press.

Poetry
ISBN 979-8-9899487-6-5

Cover Photo: *The Sacred* by C.L. Downing

Author photo: Nick Felkey, Felkey Creative Services, Bainbridge Island, WA

Book design by Tonya Namura, using Gill Sans (display) and Minion Pro (text)

MoonPath Press,
an imprint of Concrete Wolf Poetry Series,
is dedicated to publishing the finest poets
living in the U.S. Pacific Northwest.

MoonPath Press
c/o Concrete Wolf
PO Box 2220
Newport, OR 97365-0163

MoonPathPress@gmail.com

http://MoonPathPress.com

For Mark, Cooper, and Kari

You are my loves, you are my lights.

*See their oubliettes of light,
…feel their silent pull like a prayer.*
—"Crown Shyness"

Contents

Grandmother's Story Stone	3
Mother Dances the Blues	4
Sarma	5
What Cracks Open	7
A Long Time Ago There Was and There Wasn't	8
Grandfather	9
Walking Home	11
Solitaire	12
Their Boots and Spikes	13
Pork Belly	14
Three Flowers for Cynthia	16
A Single Icicle	18
Refuge	19
Brother, Your Suicide	20
Crown Shyness	21
Safety Risk	22
Letter to My Father Never Sent	23
The Rains of November Have Come Again	24
The Button Jar	25
The Blessing of the Onions	26
Milkweed	27
Iowa Night	28
Arriving in Montana, 1973	29
In the Starlite Motel	31
Venting Three Ways	32
I Gave My Son My Father's Name	33
Breaking Ground	35
Second Child	36

Night Sky	37
Quiche, a Love Poem	38
What's Broken	39
Thirst	40
I Went Out to Hear	41
Stones in the Boat	42
He Waits Inside	43
Safe Harbor	44
Full Buck Moon After My Juvie Shift	46
History Lesson on a Sunday Afternoon	48
Stayed So Long	49
Melancholy	50
Present Time	51
In the Field of Significant Moments	52
Tea Rose in August	53
Life Could Be Harder	54
Watched	55
Moss, Dandelion	56
We Are in the Lush Time	57
Singing in the Choir with My Mother	58
Evanescent	59
The Family Had Few Rituals	60
Phantom and Epiphany	61
Re-membering	62
The Trees Are Lit	63
Notes	65
Acknowledgments	67
Gratitude	69
About the Author	73

Oubliettes of Light

Grandmother's Story Stone

I know no Armenian, she no English.
Like a pupil at attention, she sits
in her straight chair by the cookstove,
shuffles pages back to front
in her Armenian Bible. She mutters,
gnarled fingers rowing.

Her black lace-up shoes clunk
back and forth across scrubbed linoleum.
Her cotton stockings sloop
into ankle bracelets. She slings onions
into her bib apron from a bushel basket.

Her sun-browned hands tuck grape leaves around rice,
pry up the stove lid, push in kindling sticks.
Her whiskers sprout from greasy wrinkles,
garlic, olive oil, mint, her perfume.
I brace for her kiss.

When she speaks with my father
my ears tune the soft guttering.
I whisper behind my hand
scubbity, scubbity, scubbity.

Memories ghost August sunlight,
slant through blinds. Stories never told
collide in the parlor, migrate
behind the curio cabinet glass door,
colonize her mementos with silence.

I beseech her opaque story stone to speak.
Like those who sucked stones
in the Syrian desert I'm thirsty for more.
Her voice roosts inside me, pricks my skin,
a straight pin lost in my skirt's hem.

Mother Dances the Blues

She opens her gold lipstick brush,
flicks it against the red wax pillar
risen from its shiny case,
outlines her mouth, fills in her lips,
smacks them together,
her kiss on a tissue
a red rose discarded.

Her music Saturday afternoons—
Glenn Miller, Harry James, Tommy Dorsey—
sends her sashaying,
snicking her tongue against her teeth
matching the rhythm heel and toe.

Weekdays she shuffles in the kitchen door at six.
We kids clamor like an out-of-control carillon.
If he is home he complains—
she failed to iron his shirt,
make the bed, sweep up.
She crosses the patched linoleum,
takes down her glass,
pours her Scotch.
Ice clinking,
ghost ship unanchored,
she slips from him,
sails out beyond us all.

Sarma

We trudge in conscripted from our play,
sit at the table and begin our work.
Father's impatience wraps around his jeers
as he shows us how it is done.

Our small fingers plug away at stacks
of brined grape leaves, rumpled, easily torn.
Each leaf pile shrinks, grows tall again
down the long afternoon.

Rice cooked in olive oil,
canned tomatoes and chopped onions
in a sticky mound
in the massive frying pan ringed with spoons.

There is a particular tension that holds the leaves,
precision in folding left and right to center.
A slight pressure rolls the rice
in the leaf without breakage.

I lick my fingers for the salt,
my secret sealed, his betrayal
wrapped in finger-thick rolls.
We stack the cigars (his name for them)
round and round in a big pot,
like mossed stones in our old well.

Of all the dishes his mother taught him
this is my favorite, fulcrum
to lost childhood time and stomachs filled.
I tuck and roll, no longer hear his voice.
The fat, green stubs stew gently
over a low gas flame.

Lemon tang fills the house.
I wait for the slick, salty morsels,
the simple comfort of warm rice.

What Cracks Open

The scalpel cuts, splits skin.
Heart muscle stills
then opens to the blade.

Pointed garden spade breaks
the ice so robins home too soon
can drink.

Rock fractures when dynamite blows,
mountain pass opens,
shards scatter.

Seed wrestles against cold earth,
nanoscopic movements rupture its husk,
tiny white shoots emerge, green up.

Ancient statues steadfast
in Roman gardens
lose whole arms to gravity.

The blue ceramic pot makes room
for the red geranium's roots to ramble
in search of water.

Hearts are breached every day—

the airport entry gate kiss,
your child's overdose,
the man on the cardboard missing a shoe,

the white wings of the cabbage moth
balanced on the purple chive blossom.

A Long Time Ago There Was and There Wasn't

*for Baizer Blanche Garabedian Jamgochian,
1885–1975*

She crouched behind the wine cask.
Doors crashed—shouts, her mother's screams,
Turkish boots pounding, pots cracking,
small brown bird vanished into desert air—

She died into silence
that held her like a shroud,
cloaked in hunger without tears.
Wind blew through her eyes.

She tipped and slid in the boat
in the dark, rumbled for days and days,
like an ancient rockslide on Mt. Ararat.
She tumbled into exile,

waterfalls of words pitched over her on the dock.
Sounds marched out of open mouths.
Dry as dust this language
she would live in for seventy-nine years

yet never speak. Lost
in her wilderness of grief,
killing the memory of the killings,
she forgot how the story went.

Grandfather

for Osker Jamgochian, 1874–1956

Your dark face shadowed
  in the small black and white photo

   who were you   what did you see
Armenian brown eyes   locked
  onslaught
      Turk militia in the village
wife and child   swords and guns

 butchered where they crouched
      too late   too late   too late

   friends dragged you
     from your cobbler shop
stitching awls   and chisels dropped

    the boats   Cyprus   Greece
New York   sea change
  three lives ended   one restarts

  cook now not cobbler
new language   Armenian diaspora
    arranged marriage
  new wife New Hampshire

pear trees   white farmhouse
      barn doors   cousins next door
        survivors
nine children born at home
             four babies die

    children to build up
the motherland
        one day we will return

the story I missed
        memories
            misplaced

Walking Home

Streetlights flick on one by one
each in its turn beaconing my small feet.
Cones of light slice through elm leaves
as evening throws its shawl around me.
Canopy rustle surefire ghost at my heels,
I pick up my pace,
night breeze tapping hairs on my neck.

Bats come out of hiding to hunt moths
against the fat yellow lightbulbs,
flying so fast I miss them,
see only the blank spots they leave
in the corner of my eye
like memories, years later,
that flit around my porch rocker in the dusk.

Those evenings when I tunneled
the darkening street were quiet times
when I skimmed ahead of the day's events,
my wishes for safety
just out of reach
like fireflies dancing in humid twilight.

Solitaire

We were fascinated
by the flutter of the cards
my father shuffled
on the faded kitchen table oilcloth
week after week
cards laid out in rows
black, red, black, red,
kings' and queens' faces
faded as antique postcards.

He played his morning games
in private reverie, his fingers gentle,
caressing each card.

We left for school knowing
he would shave, shower,
drive off to call on folks
on far-flung rural roads,
strike fear in their hearts
with his tales of catastrophes.

He sold them insurance policies
they couldn't afford yet would buy,
felled by the weight of his persuasion,
his magic-trick sales pitch,
doing in the end, like us,
what they did not want to do.

Their Boots and Spikes

Pickelhaube spikes on their helmets
the ghost soldiers come again.
They crowd the top of the stairs.
Heavy boots stomp down and down.
My three sisters and I huddle
in the back corner of the coal cellar
waiting for the metal latch to lift
on the thick oak door.
Will they find us if we stop breathing?
Yes, they will pull the light string.
I spread my body as wide as it will go
in front of my sisters. I'm sweating.

I startle awake,
alone in the small bedroom
just off the dining room,
where morning after morning
I hear his footsteps approaching.
One parent asleep, one awake
pushing the door open
across red linoleum, rubber doorstop
sliding with a soft swish,
his hands, the boots and spikes.

Pork Belly

Time to slaughter this pig.
Skin it, gut it, hack it up—
ham hocks to smoke,
tenderloin, chops, bacon.

I order bacon every time I eat breakfast out,
refusing to tether its crispy succulence
to your early morning bedroom visits.

The fry smell that woke me then
doesn't repulse me now,
the salty fat doesn't choke in my craw
like the fear that pinned me to the mattress
when your calloused hands slid
under my flannels while the others slept.

The back rub was melt-in-the-mouth
pork crackling until your heavy hands
wandered like pigs rooting for slop
around to my breast buds,
under my waistband,
down over my chamois bottom.

Like a pregnant sow I carried
my dark secret heavy in the belly.
Shame slung about me all day,
clotted mud in pigs' feet.

Morning after morning this baffling
silent backrub-not-backrub packed
streaky rashers around my waist,
crammed my never-asked questions
down my throat.

It's all mine now,
this thick square of prime belly meat,
lying under the ribs
up against my heart.

Three Flowers for Cynthia

Forsythia
First to the party flouncing a crinoline petticoat,
prima ballerina at the Annual Mud Ball.
Yellow, yellow, yellow rounds in my mouth,
pulls me out of muck that sucks
at my red rubber boots.
I watch whips of gold snap in the wind.
Our forsythia bush is yours, Mother,
slant rhyme of early spring,
a soft mass of sunlight I want to lay
around my shoulders like a feather boa.

Lilac
Neglected and gangling, the lilac hedge
thrives, pale lavender torches signal the bees.
I drink deep from ticklish tufts, swallow
fragrance like honeyed purple broth.
One whiff and I am home again
and she is bringing in an armload.
Cut, the blossoms fade fast,
tiny trumpets turn brown, droop,
harbinger of years to come.

Poppy
The Memorial Day parade wound its way
to the cemetery year after year where we heard
how poppies blow, row on row,
in Flanders Fields. Your poppies, sirens of summer
in huge crepe paper skirts danced along our driveway.
You liked bold flowers best—
zinnias, geraniums, marigolds, snaps—
decked out in red, orange, gold, magenta.

You were happy then, on your knees,
hands in the dirt, hidden away
among your friends the black-eyed Susans.

Wherever you went
down those spring and summer days,
I wanted to go with you.

A Single Icicle

Icicles lined the gutters of our house
in New York farm country.
Thick as our arms
they reached into the snowbanks below.
We plucked the smaller icicles,
sucked them until our lips turned blue,
so numb we couldn't form our words.
In those days winter arrived early,
stayed for months.

We had sword fights,
our ice blades fused to our mittens
as we became the cold.
We knocked the icicles down with snowballs,
smashing holes in the line
like a TV prison cell breakout,
our screams of triumph
when a whole wall came splintering down.

Now near the Salish Sea
winter makes its evanescent visit—
a week in February
when winds from the Fraser Valley
swoop down upon us—
it lasts just long enough for a single icicle
to form outside my window,
rainwater dripping and freezing
to make its point.

Refuge

for the children of Ukraine

On the deck this morning a baby rabbit—
as if vaulted into an Easter egg hunt.

Its cottontail points up as it dips over the edge
seeking a way off the barren wooden plain,

escape from hang-gliding eagles,
stalking coyotes and feral cats.

It dashes side to side,
zigzags in abrupt reversals

as if it can't find its way home.

Brother, Your Suicide

feels like the backhand you landed on me
that day we fought over *Gunsmoke* or *Bonanza*.

In grade school photos your scowling black eyebrows
accosted us year after year.

Girls were rats to your pied-piping charm,
your arrogance a concrete coffin

cast around your insecurities
as you strutted from crisis to crisis.

The gun spat your brain across the sheet
you hung behind the chair

in your girlfriend's new condo,
hundreds of miles from your son and daughter.

I sat in the car after the line went dead,
watched January sun shriek through clouds.

Crown Shyness

"Trees are poems the earth writes upon the sky."
Kahlil Gibran

Trees talk belowground,
web a wide net
of kin recognition in the dark.
Sisters at a reunion
they chat, feed one another, share water.

Above ground birch trees glint
white, a family gathering.
At their crowns they connect
without touching, branches
channel like braids of the Madison River.
Trees gap for safety,
disease prevention, or to avoid
colliding in storms.

It's the idea of collaboration I like most.
Sightless, they saturate forest sky.
Lying on my back I see their oubliettes of light.
In the stillness I hear them breathe for me,
feel their silent pull like a prayer.

Safety Risk

So many animals exposed at low tide—
some will burrow, others will be plucked
at random, lifted, dashed to the rocks,
downed by a hungry crow.
I watch the gull's flight over the tide flat,
notice the black blob in its beak.
Which mollusk will be breakfast?

One eats well, exercises,
is diagnosed with Stage 4 pancreatic cancer.
Another steps off a curb to cross for coffee,
hit by a car. Another shopping at Walmart,
body exploded by an AR-15.

Like the minnows in the hunting waters
of great blue herons we are here one minute,
gone down a gullet the next.

A life lived, risked, lost.
Buried or exposed,
whole or invaded,
knocked flat
or on solid footing.

Letter to My Father Never Sent

Time to break
the windowpane of silence
in that old gray house

scribbled screams
bouncing witless
against the façade of family

letter page dry as dirt
in drought covered
with ripped words
like ululating stones
cast out on rancorous waters

to leech the anger
douse grief
heart peeled like an egg

my brothers' denials of what you did
chittering in the silence
left me licking
the dried pith of an orange,
bitter.

The Rains of November Have Come Again

nailing the metal roof. It falls steady on,
clicking like a loose wheel bearing.

The brilliant reds and golds
are ripped off the trees, drenched
until they drown, mushed underfoot.

I want more of the sun's colorcalling,
less of its slantburn in my squint
where day gives way to black night by five.

I want more sweet melancholy autumn
stretched over more days,
days that could bring back the siblings

who once surrounded me with noise
jumping in giant piles of leaves we raked,
the lift of our leaps, our piercing screams,

soft landings we banked on.
I want to walk along small-town streets
lined with trees so blazed

I can't pick out a single leaf.

The Button Jar

She sits cross-legged on the rag rug,
sorts small whites, blues, greens:
four-holers from Grandpa's old shirts,
two-holed pearl buttons from sheer blouses,
shoe buttons with round leather tops and metal loops
like miniature black mushrooms.

Her favorites, what Gram calls the dressy ones:
silver buttons like woven straw baskets,
pink bows saved for her doll's clothes,
tiny red ones like wild strawberries
in the woods, amber ovals,
a yellow butterfly alone in the crowd.

She arranges them like Halloween candy,
the simple rhythm of piles, colors, shapes.
She fingers the buttons,
thumbs their shallow dips,
covers pearlescence of abalone disks
reclaimed from sweaters and worn-out dresses,
rubs them gently like tiny worry stones.

She scoops them up, puts them in the jar,
puts the jar back in its place.
The buttons live inside the sewing cabinet
with the hooks and eyes, zippers, scissors,
spools of colored thread on tilted nails.

What's left behind are the stories she tells herself—
of families that wore them, how they lived
in a big glass house all jumbled together,
like hers, needing to be seen,
needing to be sorted.

The Blessing of the Onions

Father smells of raw onion,
sun-heated peat, beer sweat.
His thick hand jerks the scallions
one by one from stony soil.
He brushes dirt from roots,
shreds the outer white-green layers,
bites it through. Molars grind
hot fibers to pulp, the flash of gold
between his two front teeth.

We thin the long row.
Onion skins and grit dust my hair.
His rants against my mother cascade
over my small bent back.
We bind the onions into bunches.
Each morning we basket them
in the hutch at road's edge.
In the humid dusk he collects coins
from the rusty coffee can,
pockets his petty hoard.
In winter the onions bushel, intimate
and silent in the wire cellar bin.

Now I slice them into medallions,
slant fractions, pungent
perfume clouds my kitchen.
The onions come each year
out of earth into body,
bring tears and succor,
blessing the sauce and stir fry.
My knife bites in peace against the wood.
Sweetness and fire feed me.

Milkweed

Monarchs, habitual companions all summer,
perch on the milkweed flower heads,
geishas waving orange and black fans
on pale pink cushions.

The pods summon me, moth to candle flames
covered in soft green barbs.
Split as fresh peas,
their flat brown seeds anchor soft white sails,
gossamer floss lining a fairy's cradle.

I scoop out the pod,
puff hard, let feathers fly
across vacant pastures,
tug pods from dusty stalks
one after another after another.

My child self knew nothing about pesticides,
endangered pollinators, the mowing
of milkweed along roadsides and railroads.
It was the feel of smooth silk,
the release I wanted,
the puff of light.

Iowa Night

She arrived from the north uninvited,
knew he would be glad to see her.

They walked the fallow railroad tracks
between tall corn rows under the moon.

The white cat followed, silent on a single rail,
the corn not yet tasseled.

They drank wine on the old porch.
He showed her to the spare bedroom

in his grandfather's house
where she slept alone then rode the train home.

That night he played his mandolin for the cat
as they waited for the moon to rise.

Arriving in Montana, 1973

Sweat-hot in the '68 black pickup truck
they clatter the washboard road
the summer of the fires.
Each day they patch the hole in the gas tank
with bubble gum chewed
while she thinks about sex
in the tent on the KOA gravel.

She escaped New York, off to the West
at 50 miles per hour, padding her losses
with cornfields, prairie grass,
tumbleweeds rattling across the tar,
puffy thunderheads above the flat horizon.

Terror-stunned from near head-ons with logging trucks
they slide out of the cab into the barnyard.
The rancher hails them,
corncob pipe jammed in the corner of her mouth.
Catching up an ax from a tree stump
she whacks the head off a chicken,
plucks it clean for her 4th of July barbeque.

Leaving laughter and beer behind,
every stranger at the fire pit a new friend,
she climbs the hill, breathes
against the rail fence.
Quarter horses nose thick green grass,
shadows sunset-stretch below,
the blue Bitterroots sail down the valley.

First stars canopy the day's memories:
so much sky, that headless chicken
running about the yard, the Stetson cowboy hats.

In her feasted famine
she places the femur knob in her cheek,
sucks and savors the marrow.

In the Starlite Motel

Under the red glow of the Vacancy sign,
we drank Boone's Farm Strawberry Hill wine,
watched Johnny Carson propped
on pillows of questionable cleanliness,
waiting until I was inebriated enough to forget
why I'd summoned him there.

Red neon lasered through the
gap in the sagging drapes.
The AC didn't work.
In the morning we notched and buttoned,
left sex-rumpled sheets that musked the room
for housekeeping, green bottles in the tin waste can.

There followed years of the manyness of beds
shared with men I can't call to mind.
Sheets worn, limp, loosed in humid rooms,
beds pillow-dented and empty.
I've passed No Vacancy signs many times,
wondered what it is like
to know a full-up love,
no room available.

Venting Three Ways

We meet for lunch,
sound off about government corruption,
our husbands, our various ailments.
We let loose over our sandwiches,
wedge doors open with torn and tired rags
newly lubricated with yesterday's irritations.
Better to vent than to stuff, we say.

Midmorning in summer the hen next door
intrudes with her Chinese water-torture call:
bawk, bawk, bawk, bawk, bawk—starts slow,
gets faster, louder. Her egg,
wrapped in the tissue of her uterus,
moves through her vent
until she pushes it out of her body.

My egg attached to the wall of my uterus,
clung there for nine months
egg to zygote to fetus to child.
I labored fourteen hours to shunt my son
down the birth canal, ten fingers, ten toes,
nearly turning myself inside out.
With no push left, they cut and released him.
His blue caul-shell torn, mouth wide to air,
he entered this world without a squawk.

I Gave My Son My Father's Name

I cast my father out when I was nineteen,
      left him behind
like a beater car in the junkyard.

Eli, *elevated, high, ascent,* a way across
      an ancient pain-chiseled chasm.
Perhaps this naming was a prayer,

a bell to ring my heart open,
      a plea for redemption, a reclamation.
I gave my son his grandfather's name,

totem to a past I don't know,
      through-thread of our heritage,
a wedge against forgetting we come

from Armenians who fled the genocide,
      maybe a declaration of survival,
sacred emblem of our kin.

Don't we cherish what comes from what is broken?
      I gave my beloved son a remnant of my father,
reminder of my father's charm,

his dark good looks,
      his big hands that built the greenhouse
with recycled windows,

planted tomatoes and green beans.
      When I gave my son my father's name
I didn't know I was asking once more

for my father's love.
        Talisman of good luck, amulet of protection,
strength, resilience, healing.

Thirty-four years ago I gave my son
        my father's name for his middle name.
Rope bridge between mother, child, old man.

Breaking Ground

When our father enters the room
we get out of his chair.
My mother serves him first—
macaroni, ground beef, boiled beans.

We pick rocks that rise out of soil each year
as if summoned from the Susquehanna riverbed.
We pull weeds, clean the soil for tomato plants,
the corner patch for squash.

I work beside him
bent under the weight
of his insults about Mother—
She smells like a dead fish down there.

I return when my son is three
reluctant to enter the storm center,
house stuffed and filthy,
the garden a wandering jungle.

We search for plant remnants
in that tired soil, walk
crooked rows looking
for stray green beans,
treasures my son spies
beneath broad leaves.
Stones ping our rusty buckets.

Dead now, the old man, his garden.

Back home my son takes small stones
from his pocket, places them
one by one in the dirt
beside his young tomato plant.

Second Child

I miscarried my second child in the toilet
while my mother-in-law died down the block.
Twenty-five years later
my husband has trouble
remembering I was pregnant.

Later, we come to the memorial garden
at the library where Dorothy volunteered.
Our niece played the cello.
My husband spoke about his mother.

My son and I held two red balloons,
one for Grandma, one for Baby.
Inside each a note:
I love you.

Grandma will take care of Baby in heaven
I told him, though I don't believe in heaven.
He stood with his head tilted back
holding my hand,
watched until the balloons disappeared.

Night Sky

When I was young and our son was small
you painted the heavens on his bedroom ceiling
in fluorescent paint so the stars would shine all night

and now when I am old and pierced with pain
you clean the house and hang the laundry
wash the dishes every night and you say

that's fair since I cook our dinner
and this love you hold for me is a boundless miracle
like the night sky I cannot do without.

Quiche, a Love Poem

Do you want the quiche? he asks,
the leftover piece from Easter brunch,
creamy with Swiss cheese,
savory with bacon and onions,
excellent flakey crust.
I say *yes, that would be good.*
Later, I understand
his generous offering to my desire.
It would have tasted even better in his mouth.

What's Broken

after Dorianne Laux

The water in the cove, cracked diamonds,
the red metal flag from the mailbox.

The ceramic bowl into shards, grapefruit
rolling everywhere. The joint in my left foot

between the calcaneus and cuboid bones.
Broken,

the sunflower head heavy-bent,
opium poppy balls leaning, petals long gone.

Years ago my father's manual single-blade
cultivator, pushing hard clay. Broken,

the birthday transistor radio my brother
hurled at the kitchen wall. *What hasn't*

been rent, divided, split? Broken,
the days into hours, the hours

down into time. I lie in bed,
count ten different birds

eating suet and seeds,
my bones fusing.

Thirst

I swing my legs over the bed,
feel the stab of pain in my right hip.
Concentrate on getting to the toilet
without leaking. Minutes pass.
I check my phone,
hobble to the kitchen,
punch the bold setting for coffee,
stand at the sink,
watch the goldfinches
vie for a perch.

Bright yellow males,
olive females, all hungry, all day.
They've emptied half the tube of seeds
since yesterday, voracious.

I am eager for my desk,
my journal, the Pastan, Kooser,
Limón poems, over and over.
The flow of words—theirs and mine—
slacks my thirst, overrides pain,
makes room for a breath.

On these days that pass without rain
the goldfinches drink often.
They come in singles and pairs—
dip their heads, drink,
look around, drink again—
little orange beaks
stabbing the water.

I Went Out to Hear

after Leila Chatti

I went out to hear
birdsong. Layered
in springblue air like icing
on cake sweet
clamor of joy,
praise song to life.
I hear the undertow of bees,
find one dancing
on the poppy's green ball
in the arms of ivory pistils,
lavender petals ten times the bee's size
wave a Victorian fan flirtation.
Standing stock still, eyes locked,
knees heavy with pollen, I'm lost,
beat fevered wings
willing to work
this singular moment forever.

Stones in the Boat

Raindrops like stones
pelt the purple asters to ground.
The pond slowly fills.
Widgeons drop in for winter.

I lugged it for years, pain
an iron anchor dragging behind,
steel buckets full of thoughts
spoken and not.

Violent acts witnessed
hoarded all this time
don't belong to me.
I give them back.

I scoop to keep from sinking,
scull to keep from drowning,
toss all the burdens over the side.
It's taken years.

Arriving at Mt. Ararat
on the forty-first morning,
I step out of the boat onto dry land,
intact.

He Waits Inside

stares out on dirt fields.
A single crow stabs the stubbled soil.
He waits, in khaki pants, white t-shirt,
the Big Yard asphalt carpet empty.

Twisted razor wire
like rolled ton hay bales,
coils along the prison's chain link fence,
bow-tie points glint in midday heat.

Tumbleweeds snicked tight
against dry pasture fence, foreheads bowed
to brown dirt clods, rounded twig-backs
tucked in silent prayer.

Red-rusted tractor caught on the ridge
wheels hooked over the sharp edge,
black paper cutout tipped like a lone drunk
against the bar, tilts over brown-furrowed acres.

All this land and sky,
the hills, folds and flats
stretch out from him, unbroken.
The red-tailed hawk in the white sky
lifts, dives, rises.

Safe Harbor

At the King County Juvenile Detention Center

The boy and I sit under bright lights.
He talks of the hardest things.
It's cold. I see him.

There is no sanctum here,
only barren walls, cold metal stools
bolted to the concrete floor.

No soft organ music, no candles,
only the flame in my mind,
a light I throw around him.

Surrounded on all sides—
guards at the post, other chaplains, other kids—
in the big open room.

He offers me the fierce defiance of the trapped,
defends the gun he carried to school every day,
jokes to keep the fox of fear at bay.

Each morning when his door lock pops
he hears a gunshot, startles
to bolt from his hole.

Brown and blue eyes lock,
forge a tiny sanctuary.
He stays on with me,
empties out his story.

Truth or manipulation?
It doesn't matter.
This is his anchor, his dock,
his time.

Full Buck Moon After My Juvie Shift

Under the full October moon
bucks bugle, begin their pointed clashes,
a doe prize to the dominant.

Moon watching, whiskey glass in hand,
I want to forget her story.

He gave her drugs, beat her that night in the car,
raped her. She shot him with his gun, ran.
He's found in the morning in the car,
pants around his ankles.

Glimmer moon sews gold seams
in the rock-mountain cloud,
bright beams burst out,
flood the gooseneck fronds,
spotlight one small white moth.

The big bucks fight, mount the does
without witness.

His gun between the seats
glints in the streetlight.
He was waving it around all night.

She's sixteen. The prosecutor charges
premeditated murder.
*She is old enough to know
what she was doing.*

She waits weeks for trial
alone with her nightmares.
It's like a crazy movie, she says.

The whiskey moon slides down like tears.

History Lesson on a Sunday Afternoon

"Four hundred years after enslaved Africans were first brought to Virginia, most Americans still don't know the full story of slavery."
                                1619 Project

Young gulls bellow
as their parents drop clams
on the rocky beach.
I walk the road edge at low tide.

Three schoolgirls trudge along
in pink BOGS boots,
whacking rocks with their sticks.
They called the Black men boys, one said.

The girls talk over one another,
comments swooping back and forth.
The light slaves got the best jobs inside the house.

*They were warm, got to eat leftovers
and they only had to clean the house.*

They were lucky.

Sticks swinging,
the girls dropped the subject.
I watched them go down the beach.

What counts for luck?
The gulls dip and soar over the tide flat.

Stayed So Long

in the summer afternoon
I fall into the blue columbine flute
bump into a bee
dance with his stripes.

The bee's story is shorter than mine
one season, six weeks;
mine, seventy years
spent traveling vines.

Brief as the blossom summer,
the bee buzzed on
unhampered by thoughts
of its death. Reverie
rising I whispered
the secret I knew:
only one life to live.
Squander it.

Melancholy

tiptoes in
on the back
of slanting
August sun
as if I won't notice,
lights the goldenrod,
its summer glory gold
nearly spent.
Day by day
song sparrows silence
their voices.

Nothing halts
its progress.
Gray rain swings
the door wide.
Pushed by chill gusts
it sweeps in,
evening cloak swirling,
claims its place
by my chair.
I light the fire.
The candle.
Take up my hot cup.

Present Time

In our absent minds we pick
at our brown spots,
his on his right temple, mine
high on my left cheekbone
under my eye
like a beauty mark.

It's one thing to notice
the bumps and aches,
another to grip each moment
in a breath, mark it—

the foolproof fragrance
of his Tartine Country loaves
on a foggy Saturday in February,

faithful heat of the first sip of coffee
silky with heavy cream—
whispers of a life shared.

In the Field of Significant Moments

The crow jumps on the edge of the road.
In its beak not a crab or a clamshell,
but a baby bird
naked and pink against the asphalt.

The chick dangles by one miniature wing,
head lolling on its cord neck.
Sparrow mother's frenzied flapping
useless as the crow's harsh screech
at the eagle that raids its nest.

No one else witnesses this death.

In the nest, heads tipped back,
beaks wide like a lucky four of diamonds,
food dealt out of the sky.

They have more hope than I,
blind faith one could call it.
Survival instinct, you say.
Yes, and isn't that also faith
in its own right?

Like swallows that swoop
among sunset mosquitos
taking their evening meal,
this feeding of one
with the sacrifice of another.

Memory plays this silent movie all day:
crow, hatchling, mother bird, human witness.
Nature incessant in its savage beauty,
the whole of it intent on life.

Tea Rose in August

How would it be to lie
in the dip of the rose petal,
stretch out along its pale curve,
take up each edge,
wrap its silken robe around my body?

How would it be to feather float
into the half-open flower,
inhale its bees-come-hither scent,
pollinating summons of indescribable lemon
cooling the senses?

How would it be to tuck
inside the butterfly's bed,
my old body swathed
in the pink glow of this cocoon?

Life Could Be Harder

I lean on my cane, wait
for the woman in a wheelchair
to roll herself up and over the threshold.
A tattoo covers her leg stump.
I'll pick up my leg on Monday,
she says at the desk.

I walk out, open the car door,
lift my braced leg in,
raise the seat with the electric lever,
put the handicapped placard
in the glove box,
start the car, drive home.

Watched

The long driveway draws me
in search of the mountain bluebird pair.

A spun-gold horse
looks up from her green banquet.

She and her chestnut companion chew,
prairie dog stands still as a fence post.

Tree swallow parents stare me down
from their house on the rail fence

below the Madison Range,
stolid, steadfast, snow-capped

above June-green foothills.
The pronghorn in the pasture,

two brown ranch dogs on the hunt,
cedar waxwings in the juniper.

I turn. Driveway to the house rises ahead,
swallows circle my slow retreat,

the golden horse frozen perfection.

Moss, Dandelion

Sphagnum moss is resilient,
able to return to life after drying
to brown dust, litter of pain and loss.

The moss greens in the wet yard,
each spring returning to life,
a rhythm I count on.

I look for a garden pocket
where I can flourish,
a place to visit across the seasons,

witness change, the comings and goings
of plants, creatures, blooms,
a place where my curiosity twirls.

I want to scatter seeds
like the dandelion blowball—
wishes carried on the wind,
achenes that fly.

We Are in the Lush Time

when the ants on the peonies tickle the buds
open, blossoms sumptuous as the flounce
of a ballroom gown giving blush
to the garden's soft air in June.

When the scout ant finds the nectar
at the base of each green sepal
she drinks, emits pheromones
all the way back to the nest.
The worker ants trail back to the fat buds
to gather sugary droplets.

There is no such thing as a whole story.

The ants are working cogs of biological
mutualism, the peonies their factory.
Once the buds lift their plush faces to the sun
the ants move on. Where do they go then?
They sting, bite or spray aphids and thrips
with acid, drink their honeydewed bodies,
toss what's left off the plant.

Singing in the Choir with My Mother

There was no rugged cross behind the altar,
only three padded chairs,
maroon with high carved backs
below a rose window,
the only color in the church.
The largest chair flanked
by two smaller ones like a king's throne.

I sat next to my mother
in the soprano section.
Dot, she was called,
was the diva soloist
though my mother's voice was sweeter.
I would look out at the congregation,
wonder about the gray-haired people below.
One Sunday we sang for a baby that had died.
I cried through every hymn,
though I didn't know the family.

When I hear the old ones today,
Rock of Ages, Abide with Me,
a lump forms in my throat.
Attending our Presbyterian church
didn't stick with me.
It was being with my mother,
the one thing we did together in those years
that made my heart light like a songbird,
and when I joined my voice with hers
all was well, a state of grace.

Evanescent

What rides
              on a snowflake
  dust particles   or pollen?
Adrift   riding a crystal drop
    steady   slow
  nowhere
      in particular to go
               snow angel
      tick tick tick
in the hush   flakes touch down
    fugitives
      they fall.

The Family Had Few Rituals

Christmas candles unboxed
smelling of dust—
choir boys, angels, reindeer—
placed on shelf and table
never match-lit, never burned,
nicked, faded, beloved.

Eggplant, lamb, tomatoes, mint,
grape leaves wrapped around rice
kettled and cooked by the father,
mouth full of his secrets
that fell into final silence with his death.

The daughter left,
walks the labyrinth of memory,
dreams of the grandmother reading her Bible
summer nights by the woodstove.
She leans over her votive,
strikes a wooden match.

Phantom and Epiphany

She crosses the country to visit him
eight days before he dies, father apparition.

She comes knowing he will never speak of it,
abuse forty years gone, hologram

hallucination. His leg, numb after the stroke,
hurts, he says, rub lotion on it.

She stands beside his bed, frozen.
She cannot touch him.

Phantom pain agitates him. A shade snaps
open. New view: his whole life a struggle.

She reaches for the tube, spreads cream.
Black wraith of her torment slips away.

He dozes. She stares at the dull yellow wall.
Peace, what he said he prayed for,

feral as a fox at dusk.
It curls around and around,

makes its bed.

Re-membering

I look at my mother in her twenties,
black and white on my desk,
her long legs a graceful A-frame scaffold
as she claims her place on the brick walk.

I knew her in days less joyful,
going to her job, returning to our hive
to carry on her drone tasks
to feed and clothe us.

Still, she watered me.
A battered kettle with a pinprick hole,
she leaked out drop by drop
down those years. Mother lived,

bore seven children, died.
Her mind, flesh, bones dismembered
into tiny particles, salt crystals, sand.
I will soon do the same.

My fragments will home in on hers,
pigeon to nest box,
collide with what she is.
Time brings our micro bits into contact

like mayflies on the Mississippi.
We enfold, are enfolded.
Our tributaries merge,
feed a great confluence.

The Trees Are Lit

after Linda Pastan

The trees are lit
from within like Sabbath candles
illuminating the cherry blossoms,
unaware they will soon be disordered
on the branch, fall to ground.
Petals flatten, melt into earth,
like fireflies blinking out
as I will tonight,
nightgown soft as those petals
slipped over my head.

Let me lie down in gratitude,
recall and decipher the day's gifts.
Allow my soul to flow for the hours
until the sun rises,
ignites the madrone tree,
a globe to hold the goldfinch
swooping back and forth all day
from light to shadow,
feeder to fountain.

Notes

Armenian folktales often begin with "*A long time ago there was and there wasn't…*"

Crown shyness is a natural phenomenon when one canopy of tree branches avoids touching another's, forming channel-like gaps. No one knows for sure if trees are trying to reduce the spread of harmful insects, protect their branches from cracking together in storms, or trying to maximize photosynthesis.

Sarma is a traditional Armenian dish of grape leaves stuffed with rice.

Eli can be translated as elevated, high (priest), ascent, my God; Hebrew origin, Eli was high priest and teacher to Samuel in the Hebrew Bible (Old Testament).

Oubliette: a deep, well-shaped dungeon with an opening only at the top.
> Etymology: French, from Middle French, from *oublier* to forget, from Old French *oblier*, from Vulgar Latin *oblitare, frequentative of Latin *oblivisci* to forget. https://www.merriam-webster.com/dictionary/oubliette accessed 8.28.24.

Acknowledgments

I appreciate the editors who published my poems in their online and print journals, sometimes in different form or with different titles.

Avalon Literary Review: "Iowa Night"

The Bluebird Word: "The Rains of November Have Come Again"

Blue Heron Review: "Safe Harbor"

Gyroscope Review: "Tea Rose," "Cracks in Everything"

The Healing Muse: "What Cracks Open"

The Journal of Undiscovered Poets: "Breaking Ground"

Juniper: "A Single Icicle"

Last Leaves Magazine: "Sarma," "Three Flowers for Cynthia," "The Story Stone," "Pork Belly," "Long Ago There Was and There Wasn't"

Last Stanza Poetry Journal: "Crown Shyness"

The Paper Crow: "Stayed So Long"

Poetry Breakfast: "The Trees Are Lit"

The Raven's Perch: "Present Time"

Sunday Mornings at the River: Poetry Diary 2024: "Refuge"

Thimble Literary Magazine: "Venting Three Ways"

The Tishman Review: "He Waits Inside"

Two Hawks Quarterly: "In the Field of Significant Moments," "Solitaire"

Wild Greens Magazine: "We Are in the Lush Time"

Willows Wept Review: "Milkweed," "What's Broken"

Young Ravens Literary Review: "Night Sky," "Evanescent"

"Cracks in Everything" and "What Cracks Open" found the best in each other and became "What Cracks Open."

Gratitude

Infinite gratitude to Bethany Reid, beloved editor, who helped me hone my poems, create this manuscript, and encouraged me to submit for the Sally Albiso Award. Your faith in me matched my enthusiasm and your feedback supported me all the way.

This collection would not have been born and raised up without the support of my community of poets, poetry buddies, and teachers who generously shared their time and skills:

- Michele Bombardier, MFA, Bainbridge Island Poet Laureate, leader of Fishplate poetry workshops. The poet who said, "So you've been bitten by the bug!" after hearing my first open mic reading and invited me to her first workshop.
- Diane Moser, first poetry buddy before I knew what that was, new friend found late in life who teaches me every day about resilience and living with humor when the body's systems are going south.
- Carol Mikoda, lifelong friend, poet, and high school band buddy (and we know what that means!) who pushed me to publish this manuscript when I lacked courage to go for it.
- Anne Kundtz, weekly poetry buddy and kindest of friends. We write to heal, to discover, to praise.
- James Crews, limitlessly kind and spiritually grounding poet, who encouraged me in all the classes I took from him. His focus on kindness and compassion as the poet's good work helped me heal and move forward.
- Joan Roger, MFA, poetry buddy extraordinaire, whose huge heart and high intelligence helped me understand how my body wants to heal.

- Lillo Way, gracious and brilliant author of gorgeous poems, who generously read and critiqued my manuscript though we didn't know each other well. I'm so glad our friendship has blossomed.
- John Willson, a Bainbridge "Island Treasure" whose detailed, thorough, kind editing of my "baby" draft poems during Covid helped in my hour of need while reminding me the world can still operate using snail mail.
- Kathleen O'Brien, colleague from another life and excellent emerging poet whose poems about grief are enlightening and profound. How lucky to reconnect in this time of our lives.
- Ronda Piszk Broatch, another wonderful MoonPath Press poet, who kindly spent precious time sharing her wisdom and creativity.
- Danusha Lamèris, compassionate poet and poetry teacher who brings her whole self to the table every time. I've expanded my view of the world with her.

I bow, in memoriam, to Sue Sutherland-Hanson who first brought me into the circle so I could discover my passion.

Boundless gratitude to my grandmothers, Blanche Jamgochian (who never spoke English) and Ora Brown, for setting me on this path long ago, and for reappearing 60 years later to bring me forward into the light. We will meet again in the great confluence.

To my mother, Cynthia, and my father, Eli, for providing for me, teaching many lessons, and loving me.

To Mark, I am deeply grateful for your love, encouragement, and razor-sharp editorial help. To

Cooper and Kari, my beloved son and daughter-in-law, for reading my poems along the way. Your support has meant the world to me. I love you so much.

To Andrew, inspiration for my first published poem, "He Waits Inside," and for how you changed my life. Love always.

Last and not least, Lana Hechtman Ayers, Managing Editor, MoonPath Press, and Tonya Namura, book designer extraordinaire. Thank you for bringing this book into the world with your beautiful press. Your respect, kindness, and professionalism will never be forgotten.

About the Author

Lisa Ashley is a Pushcart Prize nominee who descends from Armenian genocide survivors. She has spent many years listening to, and supporting, incarcerated youth. Poems can be found in *Willows Wept Review, Juniper, Blue Heron Review, The Healing Muse, Amsterdam Quarterly, Gyroscope, Thimble, Last Leaves*, and others.

She earned a BA in journalism from the University of Montana School of Journalism and a Master of Divinity from Seattle University. *Oubliettes of Light* is her first collection and was a finalist for the Sally Albiso Award, 2024.

Lisa writes in her log home among the firs on Bainbridge Island, WA, having found her way there from rural New York by way of Montana and Seattle. She navigates her life and garden with physical limitations, help from her husband, and unlimited imagination. Her garden and fir grove provide abundant joy and solace as she observes the dancing bees and acrobatic hummingbirds in the air and on the page.

www.ingramcontent.com/pod-product-compliance
Lightning Source LLC
LaVergne TN
LVHW041627070526
838199LV00052B/3265